Second Edition

Light
in the

Shadows

Meditations

While Living

with a

Life-Threatening

Illness

by Hank Dunn

ISBN13 978-1-928560-05-0

ISBN 1-928560-05-9

Printing History
First Edition
April, 1999 — 24,800
June, 2001 — 20,319
Second Edition
March, 2005 — 20,000
May, 2007 — 20,000
August, 2010 — 9,645
September, 2013 — 7,500

This book is published by:
A & A Publishers, Inc.
43608 Habitat Circle • Lansdowne, VA 20176
Toll free (855)232-4265 • Local (571)333-0169 • Fax (571)333-0167
To obtain the latest order form go to our Web site.
Web site - www.hankdunn.com • *Email* - info@hankdunn.com
Write, call or see our Web site for information on purchasing bulk copies.

Cover photo of Red River Gorge, Kentucky, by Hank Dunn
Cover design by Paul A. Gormont, Apertures, Inc., Sterling, VA

Contents

Acknowledgments

With both the First Edition (1999) and this current version, this work would not have been possible without the help of literally hundreds of people. I am thinking first of the patients and their families who have taught me so much about living with a life-threatening illness. Right up there with them are the healthcare professionals who have shared their insights with me as we, together, attempted to offer some solace. I want to thank Pat Gerkin who has applied her editing skills to make my English much more readable. She also has a great sensitivity to things spiritual.

On the First Edition I received wonderful suggestions from individuals at the following institutions: LifePath Hospice, Tampa, FL; Hospice of Boulder County, Boulder, CO; St. Jude's Medical Center, Fullerton, CA; Sibley Hospital, Washington, DC; St. Elizabeth Medical Center, Covington, KY; Geriatrics, Medical College of Georgia, Augusta, GA; Hospice of Lourdes, Binghamton, NY; Texoma Medical Center, Denison, TX. Closer to home, I have received support and valuable suggestions from my then fellow chaplains at the Hospice of Northern Virginia (now Capital Caring). Zail Berry, M.D., checked my work to make sure it was "medically correct."

On this Second Edition a few people gave me very specific suggestions. Brad Beukema and Sally Fitzpatrick took the time to read the new Part Four and made most helpful suggestions for improvement. Joanne Lynn, MD, got me thinking about the difference between "letting go" and "letting be."

Two others stand out. I have been moved by what each of them has written. So moved, in fact, that I drove across the country a couple of times just to spend some time with them. They both offered some thoughts on the new material in Part Four. Sr. Elaine Prevallet, SL, lives in Sante Fe and gave me the phrase "the idol of control." Belden Lane, PhD, in St. Louis, helped me learn about desert spirituality and the truth that the spiritual life is more about subtraction than addition.

Hank Dunn, Spring, 2005

About the Author

For more than thirty years Hank Dunn has been ministering to patients at the end of their lives and their families. He has served as a nursing home chaplain at Fairfax Nursing Center and as a chaplain for the Hospice of Northern Virginia (now Capital Caring).

Hank is a graduate of the University of Florida and of the Southern Baptist Theological Seminary in Louisville. After serving five years as a youth minister at a very traditional church in Macon, Georgia, he moved to the DC area to be a part of the very nontraditional Church of the Saviour. After work as a carpenter and directing an inner city ministry, he moved into the chaplaincy in 1983.

He is a past president of the Northern Virginia Chapter of the Alzheimer's Association. He volunteers as an on-call chaplain at the Loudoun Hospital and at Joseph's House, a home in DC for formerly homeless men with AIDS. He is a Volunteer Pastoral Associate at his faith community, Vienna Baptist Church.

To help him explain end-of-life decisions to patients and families, he wrote a booklet to hand to them so they could reflect on the issues discussed. First published in 1990, *Hard Choices for Loving People* is in its Fifth Edition (2009) and has sold over 3,000,000 copies. It is being used in more than 6,000 hospitals, nursing homes, faith communities, and hospice programs nationwide.

Hank Dunn is a frequent speaker on topics related to the end of life. For fun he enjoys backpacking, kayaking, fishing, and life in general.

Introduction

I n my more than two decades of work with those living with a life-threatening illness I have learned some valuable lessons about living in the midst of difficult situations. I have served as a chaplain in a nursing home, with a hospice program and in as hospital as well as volunteer in a home for formerly homeless men with AIDS. As difficult as it is, what seems most important is to *live each day as fully as possible*. I have seen people live a life of meaning and purpose even while severely disabled and seriously ill.

In these few pages I have gathered the most helpful insights these patients have taught me. This book is about finding hope in hopeless situations; being grateful in the midst of great losses; experiencing a connection to things eternal; living a meaningful life while considering the possibility of death; and getting to the root issues in medical treatment decisions.

In my first book, *Hard Choices for Loving People*,[1] I outlined some of the medical treatment decisions we might face. But living with a life-threatening illness is more than just medical treatment decisions, so I felt this book was necessary to expand on the emotional and spiritual struggles brought on by disease. In neither book do I try to give medical advice. I recommend discussing medical treatments with your physician and other healthcare professionals familiar with your particular case. I can only write of my experiences with specific medical cases and they may or may not be similar to the circumstances you are facing.

All the stories I share are true, but, at times, I have changed names to protect privacy.

Each of these selections is written as a meditation—some thoughts to be pondered. They are meant to be companions for those with a life-threatening illness and their families. At the end of each piece is a thought, indicated by a check mark (✔), to carry with you through the day. My hope is that these words will help you live each day fully and that you can go into the future with courage and peace.

Part **One**

Living Each Day Fully

Hope from a Life of Gratitude

> To accept our circumstances is another miraculous cure. For anything to change or anyone to change, we must first accept ourselves, others, and the circumstance exactly as they are. Then, we need to take it one step further. We need to become grateful for ourselves or our circumstances.[2]
>
> *Melody Beattie*

As I entered the nursing home room, the noise just outside the window was deafening. Construction workers were breaking up concrete with jack hammers. Seated next to the window, not ten feet from the closest jack hammer, was my friend, Mary. She was totally blind, had beautiful white hair, and often let a smile cross her lips. As soon as I heard the noise—and saw Mary right next to it—I said, "Mary! You don't have to stay here with all this noise. We can find another room for you during the day and you can come back here after the noise has stopped." She smiled, "That's okay. I kind of like it." "You like it?" I asked. And this time with a big grin she said, "It's so good when it stops."

I asked her once what it was like to be blind. She said, "It's wonderful." "Wonderful?" I repeated. "Yes," she explained. "You can learn so much being blind. I listen to talking books and talk radio. I can tell where people are in the room and what they are doing, just from their sounds. You listen so much better when you are blind." She had a way of giving thanks for what she still possessed rather than despairing over what she had lost.

If there is one attitude that can sustain us through the most difficult of circumstances, it is "the attitude of gratitude." This is the ability to give thanks for the gifts in one's life, not necessarily because of the hardships, but in spite of them. In other words, we are not grateful that we have a life-threatening illness, but we are able to give thanks *while* we have a life-threatening illness.

If I had not seen this ability demonstrated consistently over the years, I would not have believed it possible. In the midst of the most serious illnesses, people have told me they have had a wonderful life with children, grandchildren, and beautiful memories of good times. They remember the travel and fulfilling careers. Another blind patient who was wheelchair-bound—and more than 100 years old—would often say, "Isn't God wonderful?"

✔ *May my thoughts this day turn toward gratitude for all the gifts I have received, and for those I still possess today.*

Do Some Things "Just Happen"?

> Some vital impulse spared my needing to
> reiterate the world's most frequent and pointless
> question in the face of disaster—Why? Why me?
> I never asked it; the only answer is of course Why
> not?... You may want to try at first to focus your will on
> the absolute first ground-level question. Again that's
> not "Why me?" but "What next?"[3]
>
> *Reynolds Price*

Several years ago a hurricane was making its way across the Gulf of Mexico. Landfall was expected somewhere around the Texas-Mexico border. It finally came ashore south of the border. Many lives were lost, including children on a school bus. In one of the broadcast stories of this tragedy, I recall a Texan saying something like, "God really spared us on this one." We often hear survivors of disasters credit God for sparing them and sending the calamity in another direction. The horrible implication, of course, is that God chose to kill a school bus full of children instead of me... Isn't God wonderful? Don't get me wrong—we should always have a sense of gratitude for the gift of our lives. But when something as random as a hurricane misses us, I think it would be wrong to assume God steered it through someone else's hometown instead of ours.

Rabbi Harold Kushner pondered this issue of randomness after his son died of a deforming and painful disease. He gathered his reflections in *When Bad Things Happen to Good People*. Here are a few of his words:

> A change of wind direction or the shifting of a tectonic plate can cause a hurricane or earthquake to move toward a populated area instead of out into an uninhabited stretch of land. Why? . . . There is no reason for those particular people to be afflicted rather than others. These events do not reflect God's choices. They happen at random and randomness is another name for chaos, in

those corners of the universe where God's creative light has not yet penetrated.[4]

While I was a nursing home chaplain I had the opportunity to minister to a patient whose life was maintained by a mechanical ventilator and an artificial feeding tube. He was unconscious and had been for months. Although he could possibly exist in this condition for years, he was not expected to recover. His wife was very faithful in visiting him daily. They were Jewish —he by birth, and she converted from the Catholic faith of her youth. I occasionally found her with both a Jewish prayer book and a rosary. Sitting by his bed, with the noise of the breathing machine in the background, she often said to me, "I know God has a purpose for making my husband like this."

Since they were Jewish, and she was asking the question of why this horrible thing had happened, I gave her a copy of Rabbi Kushner's book to read. A few days later she gave it back to me and said she didn't like it. I was a little surprised and asked why. "He said God is not in control of everything… that some things just happen at random," she replied. I thought, isn't that obvious, just look at your husband. What on earth would a loving God hope to gain by destroying this man's brain and his ability to swallow and breathe and then suspend him between life and death on machines? She wanted no part of this thinking. She would rather have a God who intentionally did this than let go of a God who controls everything.

One of the greatest gifts granted by the Creator is our freedom to choose our own way, even if it is contrary to what is right. Likewise, the natural world of disease and disasters is also free—not that it has a mind and chooses to afflict certain people and not others. But the apparent randomness of the universe can be the dark side of this gift of freedom. And in the midst of the randomness of disease or disaster, God is present

... not necessarily causing it, but going through it with us.

It is natural to ask "Why?" and to be angry at God. In fact, it is a necessary step in moving toward acceptance and hope in the midst of a life-threatening illness. People who are forever disappointed in God and never cease to ask why God has sent this cancer… or the illness of a child … or this auto accident miss the point. These things are just the natural tragedies of life. The real question is not "Why?" The more important questions are, "What am I going to do in this circumstance? How am I going to respond?" We can hold on to the anger and hatred, or we can respond in grace and peace. We do have a choice.

✔ *Each time I am tempted to ask, "Why?", I will change the question to "What next?" or "How am I going to respond now?"*

God's Presence in Spite of the Medical Outcome

> As we come to terms with loss and change, we may blame ourselves, our Higher Power, or others. We may hear ourselves say: "Why didn't God do it differently?..." To not allow others, or ourselves, to go through anger and blame may slow down the grief process. But we may need to get mad for a while as we search over what could have been, to finally accept what is.[5]
>
> *Melody Beattie*

The scriptures are full of stories of God "failing" and not delivering the faithful ones from tragedy. A patient struggling with cancer said to me once, "Don't you think that if you just believe hard enough you will be healed?" I often refer those asking such questions to the following two scripture passages.

There is a Hebrew story of the three men the king would destroy in the flames if they did not bow down and worship his idols. They refused to bow down knowing that God could deliver them from the fire. Then they added to their trust in God to deliver them, "But if not... we will not serve your gods." (Daniel 3:17-18) Even if they weren't delivered they would continue to trust God. We could rewrite this for those facing a life-threatening illness, "I know God can heal me and save my life, but if not, I will continue to trust in the Lord." Not being healed does not necessarily mean we lack enough faith.

Paul, the Christian apostle, was plagued with some sort of physical disability or nagging medical problem. We do not know what it was, but it bothered him enough to pray for healing. He was not healed. Here is a person Christians regard as a great man of faith and his prayers were "not answered." That is, he was not healed. But he did get an answer. God said to him in effect, "I will not heal you, but I

will not abandon you either. My grace is sufficient for you."
(II Corinthians 12:8-9)

We make a mistake to assume that God is only present if we get a "good" outcome from the medical condition we prayed to be relieved from. People in the Bible occasionally didn't get their prayers answered, yet they knew that God was with them. Another mistake is to assume that our healing or the healing of someone we love is totally dependent on the size and genuineness of our faith.

There are other miracles besides physical healing, such as the miracle of having peace in our hearts. Or the miracle of being reconciled to our families. Or the miracle of approaching this illness with serenity and a sense of the presence of God. The three men stood before the furnace with full knowledge that they could perish in the flames. But that fate, that outcome, did not deter them from their sense of God's presence.

✔ *I will try to sense God's presence in spite of what I hear from the medical reports, knowing that I am connected to an eternal Source no matter what the situation.*

Hope for Forgiveness and Reconciliation

> When we forgive, we set a prisoner free and
> discover that the prisoner we set free is us.[6]
>
> *Lewis B. Smedes*

Serious illness often brings about a serious review of our lives. In that review, we often find we have some regrets about a relationship with someone important to us. Perhaps we have been cut off from a family member because of some incident years ago. I have seen family members reunited and reconciled after years of estrangement. Sometimes they can't even remember why they were cut off from one another.

Hospice physician Ira Byock often asks his patients, "If you were to die today, God forbid, but if you were to die today, is there anything that would be left undone?" A life-threatening illness forces us to assess what is really important in our lives. It is now almost a cliché, but no one ever looks back over life and says "I wish I had spent more time working." We look back and sometimes we see hurts we have received from others or have given to others. Often that which is left undone is reconciling with someone else.

Forgiveness is the way to move beyond life's hurts. Not forget them, but take them so seriously that we must practice what some consider a divine act—forgiving. Sometimes people are uncomfortable with the idea of "forgiving" someone for a horrible act. Some would rather talk about this as "freedomness." We gain inner freedom by releasing hatred, anger, and thoughts of revenge when we forgive someone.

The other side of forgiveness is to ask to be forgiven for a wrong we have done to another. We are all capable of inflicting harm. Most likely, in the course of a lifetime, each of us has hurt someone else. The way to release this burden is to ask for forgiveness.

Many books have been written on forgiveness. Lewis B. Smedes summarizes the topic:

> The most creative power given to the human spirit is the power to heal the wounds of a past it cannot change. We do our forgiving alone inside our hearts and minds; what happens to the people we forgive depends on them. The first person to benefit from forgiving is the one who does it.... Forgiving happens in three stages: We rediscover the humanity of the person who wronged us, we surrender our right to get even, and we wish that person well.... Forgiving does not require us to reunite with the person who broke our trust.... Waiting for someone to repent before we forgive is to surrender our future to the person who wronged us.... Forgiving is not a way to avoid pain but to heal pain.... We do not excuse the person we forgive; we blame the person we forgive. Forgiving is essential; talking about it is optional.... When we forgive, we set a prisoner free and discover that the prisoner we set free is us. When we forgive we walk in stride with the forgiving God.[6]

✔ *Is there anyone from whom I need to ask forgiveness? Or, is there anyone I need to forgive? Today is a good day to begin this process.*

Choosing My Response

> You may not have control over your initial reaction to something, but you can decide what your response will be. You don't have to be at the mercy of your emotions. . . . You may not be able to change your medical prognosis, but you can control the destructive emotions that can subvert your mental and physical health. For me, acceptance has been the cornerstone to my having an emotionally healthy response to my illness.[7]
>
> *Morrie Schwartz*

> The good person out of the good treasure of the heart produces good, and the evil person out of evil treasure produces evil; for it is out of the abundance of the heart that the mouth speaks.
>
> *Luke 6:45*

You could almost feel the collective pain in the room. I had joined a local support group of the Compassionate Friends. All of these twenty or so parents had lost a child. Some to disease, some to auto accidents, one to suicide, and one stillbirth.

I had been asked to speak on the topic of "Death and Spirituality." I knew this was not a group to whom I could just give pat answers. They were there because they had suffered what all of us usually consider must be the greatest wound—the death of a child. I brought a draft of some of the selections from this book. They took me to task over the term "letting go." They said they will never let go of the memory of their child, and there is not a day that goes by that they don't think of them. I felt I needed to defend myself. I explained that I meant "let go" of the anger, bitterness, and hatred over the unfairness of a death. The memory and sadness would always be there.

These people were the experts in dealing with suffering and loss. I was planning to read a piece about a woman who was grieving, sad, and angry at God and everybody. As her 95-year-old mother lay dying in a hospital, this woman thought about all the losses she had suffered, including the death of a brother and a sister when they were teenagers, the recent death of her husband, and her escape from two countries in her pursuit of freedom.

She finished her recounting of loss after loss, and we sat in silence for a few moments as I searched for words. She broke the stillness, asking, "Do you believe in God?" I said, "Yes." She then asked, "Then how come God makes some people happy and others sad?"

Now I had to decide if I could be honest with this woman. So deep were her unhealed wounds I knew there was nothing I could do or say to take away her pain. The truth is, all of us have a choice in whether we are happy or sad. I decided to be honest. I told her happiness comes from deep inside us.

She concluded, "I will never be happy then, because there is nothing happy inside of me."

Now who was I to tell this group of grieving parents that "happiness is a choice"? I decided to go ahead with my original plan and read the selection. I finished and waited for them to tell me, "You have no idea of the depth of pain and you have no choice." That did not happen.

After just a moment of silence, from around the room, they all said that one day they made the choice to engage in life again. They made the choice to find some happiness amidst the sorrow. They will always miss their child but could go on with life in their woundedness.

This idea that we have a choice in our happiness is not original with me. Viktor Frankl is the one who told us this is the "last of the human freedoms"—the freedom to choose how we will respond in any given set of circumstances. He was a Jew and a psychiatrist who learned about this freedom as a prisoner in several concentration camps during the Second World War. Hear his words:

> The experiences of camp life show that man does have a choice of action.... Man *can* preserve a vestige of spiritual freedom, of independence of mind, even in such terrible conditions of psychic and physical stress.... We who lived in concentration camps can remember the men who walked through the huts comforting others, giving away their last piece of bread. They may have been few in number, but they offer sufficient proof that everything can be taken from a man but one thing: the last of the human freedoms—to choose one's attitude in any given set of circumstances, to choose one's own way.

> [I]n the final analysis it becomes clear that the sort of person the prisoner became was the result of an inner decision, and not the result of camp influences alone.... I became acquainted with those martyrs whose behavior in camp, whose suffering and death, bore witness to the fact that the last inner freedom cannot be lost.... It is this spiritual freedom—which cannot be taken away—that makes life meaningful and purposeful.[8]

The sort of person we become is the result of an inner decision and not the result of the influences of... cancer... the illness of a child... divorce... disability.

> ✔ *When the circumstances seem to be overwhelming, I will know I have a choice in how I am going to respond. I will not blame my illness, or other people, for how I feel inside.*

Fear of Impermanence

Learning to live is learning to let go.[9]

Sogyal Rinpoche

C. S. Lewis began his classic *A Grief Observed*, with the insight "No one ever told me that grief felt so like fear."[10] He had walked the road of cancer with his wife, and in this book he reflected on his journey.

In my twenty-two years of walking with those living with life-threatening illnesses, I have noticed often the presence of fear—fear of pain; fear of what will happen to me if I die; fear of what will happen to my family; fear of abandonment—all legitimate fears. Yet a basic fear for us all, not just those who are ill, is the fear of the fact that we will not live on this earth forever... our impermanence. So deep is this fear that we go to great lengths to cover up the reality of our impermanence.

We are little different than the Egyptian pharaohs who were buried with vast amounts of worldly possessions to carry them on to the next life. Though we don't carry possessions to the grave we do try to surround ourselves with things that tell us we shall live forever. Perhaps even our constant motion from activity to activity is an attempt to cover up our impermanence. For if we really sit still, in the silence, we might be reminded that our life is limited. So we work long hours, keep the TV on, go to shopping malls, let music and chatter fill our morning commute... perhaps to avoid the silence and being alone.

And we resist change because change reminds us of our impermanence. A life-threatening illness and possible death is the ultimate change... the ultimate threat to our permanence. Sogyal Rinpoche speaks so well to this issue:

It is only when we believe things to be permanent that we shut off the possibility of learning from change. If we shut off this possibility, we become closed, and we become grasping. Grasping is the source of all our problems. Since impermanence to us spells anguish, we grasp on to things desperately, even though all things change. We are terrified of letting go, terrified, in fact, of living at all, since learning to live is learning to let go. And this is the tragedy and the irony of our struggle to hold on: not only is it impossible, but it brings us the very pain we are seeking to avoid.[9]

✔ *I will try to see the impermanence of things as a sign of freedom. If I know all things change, I can let go and not have to grasp on to them so tightly.*

Pain and Suffering

The Hebrew way of looking at humans is that we "are a soul," not that we possess a soul. Body, soul, and spirit are so intertwined that it is difficult to know where one begins and the other ends. Being sick and in pain can make us feel emotionally down and spiritually challenged. Fortunately, there are medications and treatments that can be used to lessen the effects of pain. But when pain is present we are faced with a difficult emotional and spiritual challenge.

The Psalms often present a picture of someone in anguish. The writers of these words seek relief from their oppressions. That is their prayer. The real movement of faith is to say, "I have become like a broken vessel.... But I trust in you, O LORD; I say, 'You are my God.'" The miracle is to maintain faith in spite of the pain. This does not mean to accept pain as inevitable.

Along with aggressively using medicine to alleviate pain we might find other ways of addressing the suffering. We know some patients feel the anguish is eased after a visit with a spiritual counselor or close family member. Prayer, meditation, and visualization bring relief to some patients. Yet others are lightened after reconciling with a family member. And still others need a sense of being forgiven by someone they love or by God.

It is not a sign of weakness to seek relief from pain. Nor is it a lack of faith to be emotionally and spiritually distressed if we experience pain and suffering. In the end, we hope we can still conclude, "I trust in you, O LORD; I say, 'You are my God.'"

✔ *As I seek relief from pain through medical solutions, may I also find relief from suffering through the healing of my emotions and spirit.*

Giving Up and Letting Go

Giving up implies a struggle —
  Letting go implies a partnership
Giving up dreads the future —
  Letting go looks forward to the future
Giving up lives out of fear —
  Letting go lives out of grace and trust
Giving up is a defeat —
  Letting go is a victory
Giving up is unwillingly yielding control to forces
    beyond myself —
  Letting go is choosing to yield to forces beyond
    myself
Giving up believes that God is to be feared —
  Letting go trusts in God to care for me.

Hank Dunn

A man with AIDS once told a counselor friend of mine, "I finally learned the difference between giving up and letting go." I thought a lot about what he said and I thought about my observations of people who have fought with life-threatening illnesses. When I wrote these words, I thought I wrote them to help other people let go of people they loved. It turns out I wrote them for me, too. I have meditated on them in the aging of my own parents, raising my teenage children, coping with the normal hassles of daily life, and enduring losses that have caused deep wounds. These words are for all of life.

I once spoke on the topic "Cancer and Spirituality" to a Life With Cancer support group at a local hospital. Those in attendance were in various stages of treatment, and all were hopeful of a cure. From my work in a nursing home and at a hospice, I had built a career of telling people it is okay to let go and die in peace. As I stood in front of this group, I realized these people didn't want to hear about a peaceful death; they wanted to be cured. When I consider the role of spirituality in healing I recognize that the same spirituality that allows us to die peacefully also allows us to seek healing.

We can "let go" and still be seeking a cure. I like to think this letting go is like holding a coin in my hand. I know if I open my fist with my hand facing down, the coin falls to the ground.... I let go and lose my possession. Or, I can face the palm of my hand upward, open my fist, and the coin stays in place. I can let go of the tension of a clenched fist and still have my possession. Of course it can also be knocked out of my hand and otherwise be lost, but I have let go of control.

Patients often assume that if they just hold on they will stay alive, and if they let go they will die. There is some truth to this. I have seen people "hold on" beyond all expectations. But "letting go" can allow us to be cured as well as allow us to die peacefully. Letting go releases the tension and anxiety of holding on out of fear. Many people let go and do not die. In the process, their life gains the quality of peacefulness.

✔ *Though I resist giving up, I can learn to let go and live a life marked by peacefulness since I no longer need to grasp control.*

Part *Two*

Walking the Valley of the Shadow of Death

Through the Wilderness

> Thus says the LORD, who makes a way in the sea, a path in the mighty waters: Do not remember the former things, or consider the things of old. I am about to do a new thing; now it springs forth, do you not perceive it? I will make a way in the wilderness and rivers in the desert.
>
> *Isaiah 43:16, 18-19*

We were told to take off our hospice name tags before entering the home because the wife didn't want her husband to know he was dying. On my one and only visit into the home, the man appeared yellow because of the progression of liver cancer. Even his eyes were yellow, and it turned out he was within days of dying. When I first walked into the home, I sat alone with the wife in the living room. She was very comfortable talking about her husband's impending death. I asked her, "What is all this about not wearing our pins or talking about death? Does your husband know he is dying?" She said, "Oh, yes, he knows he is dying." I asked, "How do you know he knows?" She responded, "Because he asked me." I asked how she responded to him and she had told him, "Not while I'm around."

I suggested, "What if you had said, 'Yes, you are dying and I'm going to miss you. We have had a wonderful marriage and I love you.'" She said, "I couldn't do that. That would be too painful."

Living in the shadow of a life-threatening illness is difficult. Worse yet, when it becomes clear that there is going to be no recovery, we naturally resist any thought of what really lies ahead. Understandably, this wife wanted to avoid such a painful discussion. That is why we have such a strong urge to deny the reality of the incurable nature of the disease. We want to avoid the emotional pain of saying good-bye. The man died while his wife was at the grocery store—remember she said, "Not while I'm around."

Going through the final stages of an illness as if the patient is not going to die is to live with dishonesty between patient and family. We can't experience as much closeness as we might want if we choose to withhold part of ourselves from each other. Perhaps the only way to experience the closeness we so desire is to be open and honest. Only by acknowledging the incurable nature of the disease can we be freed to live life fully.

Denying the reality of the terminal phase of a disease is normal, expected, and perhaps even necessary. It gets us through the initial shock of such a fate. Acknowledging the truth may cause anger and depression, which are, again, normal responses.

Facing the reality of death is like encountering a wide river that must be crossed. Often people choose never to cross that river. They would rather not experience the pain. None of us can force another across. If we choose to cross the river (to face the reality of death), we move through the anger and depression. Ancient peoples knew this territory as wilderness. The wilderness is… well… "wild." It is the unknown. Dark things lurk there. But without the wilderness experience, God's people would never have moved into the promised land after they passed through the waters.

After the wilderness of grief, anger, or depression, we can move toward acceptance and hope. We can gain a sense of meaning and purpose. We can experience a closeness with our families we could never have had if we continued to deny the reality of the end of the disease.

The father of a twenty-nine-year-old son who died of leukemia told me, "I lived in denial of the certainty of my son's death to the very end. I was completely surprised when he died. I feel so guilty about that denial." I thought guilt was a strange feeling for such a natural response as denial, so I asked him about that. He said, "I felt guilty because if I had accepted that he was dying, there were so many other things I would have said to him, but I lost that opportunity."

> ✔ *When I am ready to acknowledge the reality of the future of my illness, I will begin the process of an open and honest discussion with my family.*

For Everything a Season

> For everything there is a season,
>   and a time for every matter under heaven:
>   a time to be born, and a time to die;
>   a time to weep, and a time to laugh;
>   a time to mourn, and a time to dance;
>   a time to seek, and a time to lose;
>   a time to love, and a time to hate;
>   a time for war, and a time for peace.
> *Ecclesiastes 3·1-8*

I've always had a problem reading the Ecclesiastes passage. After all, it seems like a guarantee for weeping, mourning, losing, hating, going to war and yes... dying. Who needs this? I would rather avoid these things. I also would like to know there is a God who is going to protect me from all these negative events. Yet this biblical writer makes them a part of life. Can we not have love without hate; peace without war; dancing without mourning; birth without death? We, of course, are struck with the absurdity of "birth without death." It is a universally accepted truth that there is "a time to be born, and a time to die." We do not resist the reality of death—only its timing.

I was visiting with a woman whose husband had died two months before. She was experiencing deep, painful—though appropriate—grief. She told me, "Grief is the other side of love." She had learned the biblical lesson that there is a time for everything. As painful as her mourning was, it would not even have happened had there not been love in the first place. Without love, this man's death would have been just another death announcement tucked away in the local section of the paper. But because they had loved deeply and at length, her pain was equally deep and long.

Kim was thirty-six and suffered from an advanced stage of cancer in her throat and neck. She had a fifteen-year-old daughter, Sarah, from her first marriage and a seven-year-old son, Tommy, from her most recent marriage. The local abused women's shelter was providing an apartment to help Kim escape with her children from the son's father. She was putting her life back together when the cancer struck.

Two months before she died, Kim chose to undergo some emergency surgery that would not cure her but might keep her alive a while longer. After the surgery, Sarah wrote an upbeat letter to her mother encouraging her, "Get better. I know you can beat this. You'll be home soon." Kim never again left the hospital and all the professionals involved with the case were concerned about Sarah's unrealistic expectations about her mother's recovery. Kim herself had always talked only of recovery and healing, and now her daughter was picking up this banner of optimism.

About a month before Kim's death, I ran into her daughter in the corridor at the hospital. We sat down on a couch. I wanted to open a conversation about her mother's certain death, but I feared what Sarah's reaction might be. I started the discussion with a simple, "What's going on?" She said, "You know what bothers me is that I am going to have to move to another city, leave my friends here, leave basketball, leave chorus, leave my job . . . and I am going to miss all them."

She had already begun her grieving process, which, in addition to the great loss of her mother, included mourning the loss of her life as she knew it. She went on to tell me, "When Mom was first diagnosed with cancer last year, I said to myself, if she dies I want to die too, because I don't want to live without her. I don't believe that anymore. I want to make something of my life so my Mom will be proud of me." I suggested that she might tell her mother this and how much her mother has meant to her. I suggested that Sarah thank her mother for all the lessons her mother taught her. She might even tell her mother good-bye and that it is okay to go. Tears came to Sarah's eyes, and she said she didn't think she could do it.

A couple of weeks later, Sarah and her grandmother traveled to spend a week with the relatives with whom Sarah would live. When she returned to her mother's bedside after the trip, Sarah told her, "Mom, everything is going to be okay. I am going to have a good life in my new home. I am going to be fine. You can go now." Kim died peacefully a few hours later. Sarah had accepted the fact that there is a time to die and a time to mourn. She was ready for both. This fifteen-year-old, who had been abandoned by her father, saw her mother abused by her stepfather, and now watched her mother slowly deteriorate before her eyes, was able to gather the inner strength to let go.

✔ *When the time is right, I want to be willing to move into mourning, and weeping, and even toward dying. Though it will be sad and difficult, I can accept this as a normal part of the life process.*

"Chaplain, I Don't Think I Am Ready . . . ."

> Being "ready to die" does not mean we will not
> have sadness in leaving this world. It means we
> will know it is okay to leave. We can have a calm
> assurance that our future and the future of those we
> love is secure.
>
> *Hank Dunn*

I walked into her living room and found Marilyn as I had on previous visits. She lay in the hospital bed in the middle of the room. The oxygen was running and she had her usual sad expression. Marilyn was fifty-nine, mother of two, and grandmother of three. The mother of her grandchildren is in jail, so Marilyn and her husband were granted custody and had been raising them. Marilyn was dying of lung cancer.

Her first words on my arrival were, "Chaplain, I don't think I am ready to die." As a minister I wanted to help her draw upon the resources from her strong religious faith. I thought her concern could be addressed by assuring her that she would be cared for after she died. She indeed believed she would be with God. She was "ready to die" in the sense of being ready to meet her Maker.

But I knew she still was uneasy and extremely sad. I thought back to our other conversations and knew that being ready to die is not just about having assurance that *she* will be okay after she dies. It is also having a belief that *those she leaves* behind will be okay. She loved her grandchildren dearly and she worried about their future. She knew her husband also loved his grandchildren and would continue to provide a good home for them. Yet she still worried.

Being *ready to die* has two distinct, though related, focal points. On the one hand, we must have the sense that after we die *we will be okay*. I have met people with no professed religious faith who do not believe in life after death and are comfortable with this part. Most people do feel that life will continue beyond the grave. The religious beliefs of many people help them have an assurance that they will be cared for after they die. They have a faith that they will be with God and also with those who have died before them. They can let go and trust God to care for them after death.

On the other hand, being ready to die means we also must have the sense that the future of *those we leave behind will also be okay*. I have observed over the years that those who have no children or grandchildren seem to have an easier time letting go than others. Dying and leaving behind small children is especially difficult. But being able to die at peace about those we leave behind is the same act of trust and letting go that helps us be at peace with our future in eternity. Being "ready to die" does not mean we will not have sadness in leaving this world. It means we will know it is okay to leave.

✔ *I will find ways of being assured that my future and the future of those I love will be secure.*

The Eternal Breaks into Every Day

> To me, living beyond the grave is a small part of my life of faith. It is just the logical conclusion of being connected to the eternal in my everyday life.
>
> *Hank Dunn*

I was forced to revisit the question of why I believe in God and life beyond the grave. It snuck up on me one day.

I drove to the home of the widow of one hospice patient. She lives within sight of the Blue Ridge mountains in the rolling hills of Virginia. Her husband had died two months earlier, and I wanted to check in on her. As I walked into her home she said, "Let me get my daughter. She wants to talk to you. She's a skeptic." She then stepped out back and signaled to her daughter, who was on a tractor mowing.

Almost as soon as her daughter walked into the house she began, with tears in her eyes, "I don't believe in God. I don't believe in heaven. I think religion has just made this stuff up to deal with the horrible fact that once we are dead, that is it. There is nothing beyond the grave. And that has got me so upset about my father." She continued to cry softly.

I was caught off guard a little. I expected to have a nice, easy conversation with a grieving widow and instead I had to deal with the most basic of our human questions. She was crying, and I was searching for the right words. I knew I probably would not convince her to believe in God or heaven in our brief conversation. And I didn't think I could convince her that her father was okay. But I wanted to say something… anything, that could stop her crying and ease her pain.

I told her that her sorrow probably was doubled because she was experiencing her father not only as gone from her presence but gone forever. That is a heavy burden to bear.

We spoke for a while and she did stop crying, but I knew her double sadness remained even as I left.

For days I thought about our conversation. I asked myself the question, "Why *do* I believe in God and in life after death?" It had been over twenty-five years, going back to my college and seminary days, since I challenged such a core belief. In what is too typical of me I thought of more things I wish I had said in my visit. So I wrote a letter to these women about my further reflections. Here is part of what I wrote:

> My own belief in a life after death grows out of my life connected with God now. To me, living beyond the grave is a small part of my life of faith. It is just the logical conclusion of being connected to the eternal in my everyday life. Each day I begin with a sense of being in touch with God and try to live as if that were so throughout the course of my life. It is not a big leap to believe that my spirit, the *real* me, will live on forever (in what form I do not know). I feel so alive and joined to God and the universe now, how could I not go on?
>
> If the doubts you raise are right and nothing exists beyond the grave, then I am no worse off. All cultures throughout the ages have embraced a sense of the divine and of life eternal. Perhaps I *have* lived an illusion. But it is an illusion that has made the quality of my life so rich I am willing to take that risk. For me, a life of faith is the only life of integrity I could live.
>
> I do not think this is baseless faith. I have enough evidence in my life to keep me grasping for the hand of God for a long time to come. Where do I see the fingerprints of the eternal? Explain love otherwise, or the ability to overcome hurt, pain, and anger. Explain how grace and gratitude fill a person's soul, or the resurrection of hope in a hopeless world. Look at the sun setting behind the Blue Ridge. Explain forgiveness, or reconciliation in South Africa, or Viktor Frankl in a concentration camp hearing "I am here—I am here—I am life, eternal life." Moments of each day I feel connected beyond the grave. So when I take my last breath I feel assured I will be welcomed. Now I am at home in God's world and shall be then.

Her questions helped me greatly. Perhaps my answers helped her a little.

The Frankl story I referred to touches on seeing things eternal in our everyday lives. A woman was dying in a concentration camp, and some of the inmates asked Frankl to speak to her and try to comfort her. He writes:

This young woman knew that she would die in the next few days. But when I talked to her she was cheerful in spite of this knowledge. "I am grateful that fate has hit me so hard," she told me. "In my former life I was spoiled and did not take spiritual accomplishments seriously." Pointing through the window of the hut, she said, "This tree here is the only friend I have in my loneliness." Through that window she could see just one branch of a chestnut tree, and on the branch were two blossoms. "I often talk to this tree," she said to me. I was startled and didn't quite know how to take her words. Was she delirious? Did she have occasional hallucinations? Anxiously I asked her if the tree replied. "Yes." What did it say to her? She answered, "It said to me, 'I am here—I am here—I am life, eternal life.'"[12]

✔ *Today I will look for signs of connection with things eternal so that it won't be so hard to see them when life forces me to look for them when I am seriously ill or grieving.*

Between Hope and Reality

> Denial is a protective device, a shock absorber for the soul. It prevents us from acknowledging reality until we feel prepared to cope with that particular reality.... We do not let go of our need to deny by beating ourselves into acceptance; we let go of our need to deny by allowing ourselves to become safe and strong enough to cope with the truth.[13]
>
> *Melody Beattie*

Can we pray for a miracle when no reasonable person would think one could happen? Are we showing a lack of faith if we accept the reality of a terminal diagnosis and pray for a peaceful death instead of a cure?

I have seen people struggle with these questions and their answers. One patient was a fifty-seven-year-old man who had a brain tumor. His wife had told me she could only pray for a miracle that her husband be healed. I was visiting one day and I asked the patient, "Do you pray?" He said, "Yes." I asked, "What do you pray for?" He said, "I pray for peace." His wife heard his words and as she and I walked down the stairs she said, "That's not what I am praying for. I'm praying for a miracle." I told her, "I know, and that is okay." He was in a different place than she was at the time.

The families of a couple of my patients informed me on my first visit in their homes that "God has spoken to me and said that the patient would not die but be completely healed." They went on to say they did not want any negative talk about death or dying.

One of these patients was in her twenties and had a brain tumor. I asked her, as she lay flat on her back in a hospital bed in the middle of their living room, "What are your hopes for the future?" She said, "I want to go to medical school." I said, "That is quite a goal." I was not there to convince her she was dying. I did take the parents aside to discuss what I thought was the probability of their daughter dying. They later told the nurse they didn't want me back in their home because I was too negative. Their daughter died a few weeks after my visit.

The other patient was a woman in her fifties, who had cancer in several of her vital organs. Her husband was the one most convinced of the miraculous recovery in store for his wife. I was alone with the wife on one visit when she said through her tears, "I am afraid if I die I will be disappointing my husband." Later I talked with both of them after they learned of the spread of the disease that would eventually kill her. For the first time the husband said he knew his wife could possibly die, but he still felt confident that she wouldn't. He asked if that was okay. I said, "Sure, it is okay to hope and pray for a miracle. I have two concerns, though. One is if you refuse to treat pain symptoms. The other is that you may miss saying some very important things to one another if you have removed the possibility of death from your future—things like saying how much you love one another, or asking for forgiveness, or looking back over your life together with fond memories."

Because of my experience with the parents who refused to allow me into their home again to visit their daughter, I moved slowly with this man. When his wife slipped into her final coma, I stopped by their home to give the husband a framed copy of my poem, "Giving Up and Letting Go." I could tell he was angry and still did not want to entertain the thought of his wife dying. A few days later, during his wife's final hours, he told the nurse, "Tell Hank I am sorry for being so angry at him." The woman died peacefully with her husband at her side.

The shadow cast across a life-threatening illness is the possibility of death. Although this shadow exists in all our lives, those with a life-threatening illness must confront it most directly. Thousands of years ago the psalmist wrote, "I walk through the valley of the shadow of death." Even with all modern medicine has to offer, this basic truth has not changed over the centuries.

There is no magic contained in the words *death* and *dying*. Refusing to think or speak about death will not prevent it from happening. And to allow a discussion about dying will not hasten its approach. The timing of a death is a great mystery to me. But I am convinced that allowing or avoiding a discussion about death has *absolutely nothing* to do with whether a person will actually die or be miraculously cured.

But allowing or avoiding such a discussion *will have a great impact* on the nature of a death or the nature of a healing. In general, the people who avoid talking about death and dying make the experience more painful than it need be. Those who do entertain its possibility have the most meaningful and peaceful experience. Even those who are cured of a life-threatening illness have a more meaningful life as a result of considering the possibility of dying in the midst of their illness.

Families, and sometimes physicians, say they do not want to talk about the possibility of death and dying because they don't want the patient to give up hope—meaning "hope" that the patient will not die. I say there are other things to hope for as someone is dying. Hope that the death will be peaceful. Hope that whatever has been left unsaid over the years can be said now. Hope that whatever days one has left can be lived to the fullest.

> ✔ *When the time is right I will open myself to the possibility of death and discuss it with my family. I can then live each day to the fullest as I consider that this day may be my last, or the last of someone I love. I will not miss today's opportunities for telling those I love how much they mean to me.*

Meaningfulness in the Darkest Shadows

> A man who has learned how to die has unlearned how to be a slave. [14]
>
> *Michel de Montaigne (1533-92)*

We can learn much from the lives of those who lived in concentration camps. During the Second World War, millions of people were herded into these camps to wait for death. The literature that came out of their fight to survive bears a message for those who walk in the shadow of a life-threatening illness. If those who lived in these camps could find meaning and hope, surely we can.

Etty Hillesum was a twenty-seven-year-old Jewish woman living in Amsterdam when she began to record her thoughts in journals and letters. For two years she recorded her reflections on her experiences of persecution in Amsterdam and the Westerbork concentration camp. She died in Auschwitz in 1943 at the age of twenty-nine. Even certain death did not diminish her sense of the meaningfulness of life. Hear her words:

> I feel sure that life is beautiful and worth living and meaningful. Despite everything. But that does not mean I am always filled with joy and exaltation. I am often dog-tired after standing about in queues, but I know that too is part of life, and somewhere there is something inside me that will never desert me again.
>
> I have looked our destruction, our miserable end, which has already begun in so many small ways in our daily life, straight in the eye and accepted it into my life, and my love of life has not been diminished. I am not bitter or rebellious, or in any way discouraged. I continue to grow from day to day, even with the likelihood of destruction staring me in the face.

The reality of death has become a definite part of my life; my life has, so to speak, been extended by death, by my looking death in the eye and accepting it, by accepting destruction as part of life and no longer wasting my energies on fear of death or the refusal to acknowledge its inevitability. It sounds paradoxical: by excluding death from our life we cannot live a full life, and by admitting death into our life we enlarge and enrich it.[15]

For over twenty years I have watched people live with life-threatening and terminal illnesses. Often, but not always, they have a sense of the beauty of life in spite of their current condition. From my patients, their families, and people like Etty Hillesum, I have learned it is possible to live a meaningful life in seemingly hopeless circumstances.

✔ *I will search for meaning and purpose in my life each day in spite of the circumstances.*

Part *Three*

The Heart and Soul of Medical Decisions

Quality Not Quantity

> God, give us each our own death,
> the dying that proceeds
> from each of our lives:
>
> the way we loved,
> the meanings we made,
> our need.[16]
>
> *Rainer Maria Rilke*

I want to go for quality, not quantity," my Aunt Nell told her physician when he offered her another round of chemotherapy to slow the cancer that was spreading throughout her frail body. In the past she had fought the disease, but now she knew it was time to change the focus from fighting death to living life. Although she was weak, she continued to see friends, go to church, and visit with her family. Eventually she had to be moved into a nursing home to spend her final days. My cousin Ben, and other family members, sat by her bedside for many long hours. They talked; they laughed; they reminisced. From her bed, Aunt Nell occasionally joined in the conversation and smiled often. She died peacefully.

At her funeral service, I concluded my eulogy by saying a few words about the particular gentleness and peacefulness of her last days, and really her last two years:

> I have walked this journey at the end of life with hundreds of patients and families. My own experience is, and the research shows, that we tend to die the way we lived. The peacefulness of our death is determined to a great degree by the peacefulness and acceptance with which we have lived our whole lives. The peacefulness of Nell's last days were not by chance or even because God willed it to be that way. These last days were the result of choices Nell has made over the last months and years. She wanted quality over quantity, and Ben honored her wishes for a peaceful and gentle death. The gift his mother gave him and he to her was only possible because of a life lived in peacefulness, gentleness, and letting go throughout the whole of it and not in just these last days. Nell's last days were an exclamation point on a life of grace, well lived.

Daniel Callahan writes,

> What, I wondered, have been the common traits of those people whose peaceful deaths I have seen or heard about? One point stands out: their peaceful death did not seem a matter of good fortune only. They did not die differently from the way they had lived. It was as if they gathered into one culminating moment all those personal traits and virtues that had served them well in life.... Most of all, I sensed, they put death in its place, downplaying its importance and drama.... How we die will be an expression of how we have wanted to live, and the meaning we find in our dying is likely to be at one with the meaning we have found in our living.... [A] person who has learned how to let life go may have not only a richer and more flexible life, but also one that better prepares him for his decline.[17]

Using aggressive medical interventions such as mechanical ventilators and resuscitation attempts when death is inevitable may prolong the dying process and can make it more painful and burdensome. Some people feel that "fighting to the very end" is a way of conferring meaning on their lives.

Consider another way of looking at the dying process. When a disease or injury is moving inevitably toward death, we can affirm the value of our life by graciously accepting this course. We are saying that the meaningfulness of our life stands on its own. We can die in grace and peace. We can let go. In my opinion, *that* is a meaningful life and a meaningful death—being able to spend our final days without the ICU, without machines, or without various tubes, any of which can cause a distortion of the dying process. We can let go without an effort to control the process, because we have enough inner strength and peace to die gently.

✔ *My life can have great meaning even if I don't fight death at every turn. This meaning comes from deep inside of me. A gentle and peaceful death begins by living today with gentleness and peace whether I am ill or in good health. Let this day be so lived.*

Shaking Our Fist at God

> God, give us grace to
>   accept with serenity
>   the things that cannot be changed,
>   courage to change
>   the things which should be changed,
>   and the wisdom to distinguish
>   the one from the other.[18]
>
> *Reinhold Niebuhr*

Perhaps we have been lulled into thinking that modern medicine will make sickness and death optional. We have antibiotics to fight off infections, feeding tubes to nourish those who cannot eat, and mechanical respirators to breathe for those whose lungs have failed. We even have a standing order against death—Cardiopulmonary Resuscitation (CPR). Many believe CPR can restart any heart that stops, yet we know there are large categories of patients for whom the procedure is rarely effective.

Once, everyone knew that when breathing failed, or a patient stopped eating, or when a heart was silenced, death was at hand. At times today, these conditions can be reversed and life restored by the use of heroic treatments and machines. Because they are occasionally effective does not mean such extreme measures are always required. For many patients, these conditions cannot be reversed. In earlier years, we might have said, "God had called a person home" when the heart and breathing stopped. Today, some think that this need not be the case.

People occasionally tell me that they cannot order the removal of a respirator or feeding tube or withhold CPR because to do so would be "playing God." They genuinely fear that making a decision to allow a natural death would be assuming God's role—choosing the timing of a death.

But isn't it curious that we might feel we are "playing God" when we *turn off* a machine and not feel the same fear when we *turn on* a machine? What greater message could God give than for a heart to stop, for breathing to fail, or for the ability to eat diminish? I am not saying that we should *never* use machines. They can benefit some patients greatly.

My friend, Carol Taylor, R.N., Ph.D., points out that to use medical procedures inappropriately is to shake our fists at God and to shout, "I will not accept the fate every other human before me has had to face. Although it remains clear that the use of aggressive medical procedures will not stop me from dying, I will do it my way." To relinquish control is difficult, because we have been working our whole lives to gain mastery over our world. When we use medical interventions that offer no hope of recovery, we may be shaking our fist at God and saying, "I am in control here."

✔ *Although sometimes it is not totally clear when to withhold or withdraw a medical procedure, I will try not to force my own will in a situation when all the signs point toward letting go.*

The Necessity of Grief

> I let myself experience the grief, the sadness, the despair, the bitterness, the anger, the dread, the regret, and the sense of finishing before my time. I let the tears flow until they dry up. And then I start to think about what I'm crying about. I'm crying about my own death, my departure from people I love, the sense of unfinished business and of leaving this beautiful world. Crying has helped me gradually come to accept the end—the fact that all living things die.[10]
>
> *Morrie Schwartz*

The man could not speak one intelligible word but could sing with clarity. William was a big, strong man until the day he had a stroke as he was lifting bags of fertilizer into his car at the home improvement center. Because half his body was paralyzed, he was confined to a wheelchair at the nursing home where I was chaplain. He tried to make the best of a difficult situation. He attended many activities. The nurses flirted with him, much to his delight. I was always moved when he sang loud and clear in the worship services. His verbal communication had been stripped from him, except for being able to sing plainly.

He usually wore a smile, but occasionally he experienced periods of depression. I would sit next to him and try to guess what made him so sad. Then he would tell me. With his good hand, he would lift his paralyzed hand and forearm off the tray table and let it fall limp. He looked at it with tears in his eyes. The man was grieving over the loss of the use of half his body.

Loss of our health is worthy of grief. Most of us expect people to cry, to mourn, to grieve after the death of a loved one. We would be surprised if they didn't. But grieving *in the midst of* a life-threatening illness may surprise us. Not only the patient grieves, but a family member may say, "Why am I so sad? This person I love is not dead, I should be glad he is still alive."

But look at the losses that may be associated with a life-threatening or chronic long-term illness: loss of independence; loss of a long-range future; loss of control; loss of the ability to walk; loss of appetite; loss of the control of bodily functions; loss of speech; loss of energy. Our human response to loss is grief.

Grieving is a necessary step toward finding acceptance and hope in the midst of a life-threatening illness. Understandably, we may want to block thoughts about the possibility of loss and death because such thinking brings sadness. The irony is that only if we allow ourselves to experience the pain of grief can we move on to the peace of acceptance and hope for living each day fully.

The consideration of medical treatment decisions confronts us with our losses and, therefore, brings on grief. To contemplate not attempting to resuscitate a patient reminds us that at some point this person will die, and there is nothing we can do about it. Thinking about the withdrawal or withholding of a mechanical ventilator reminds us of the loss of the ability to breathe without artificial help, and we can do nothing to stop it. To consider the withholding or withdrawal of artificial hydration or nutrition reminds us of the loss of the ability to swallow. And we can do nothing to stop an approaching death.

Some people refuse to even discuss such treatment options because it is too painful. These discussions serve as reminders of losses, so to avoid the pain they avoid the conversation. By avoiding the emotional pain today, we only postpone it until tomorrow. Regrettably, avoidance today also may cause more physical pain for the patient in the future.

When the time is right, and we have moved into our grieving, we are able to make the medical treatment decision that can assure us of a comfortable and dignified death. I had an aunt who had been struggling with breast cancer that eventually invaded other parts of her body. Her physicians offered her little hope of stopping this disease with yet another round of chemotherapy. She called me wanting to know about hospice. I explained all the benefits of hospice care for her and her family. She said she would think about it. A few days later, I came home from work to find this message from her on my answering machine, "Hank. Please give me a call. It's my time." She called hospice eventually and weeks later died peacefully at home surrounded by her family.

✔ *Today, in my sadness, I grieve for the losses brought on by illness. Experiencing the grief, I can move on to living as fully as possible.*

Making Decisions for Others

> Honor your father and your mother, so that your days may be long in the land that the LORD your God is giving you.
>
> *Exodus 20:12*

How do we honor our parents toward the end of their lives? Or honor our spouse or anyone else who depends on us to make a medical decision for them? Is the answer that we show them honor by keeping them alive at all costs? Perhaps not.

One way we can show honor is by honoring their wishes about medical interventions they may or may not want at the end of life. I was talking with the daughter of a dementia patient as she faced the decision of whether or not to insert a feeding tube in her mother. I asked her, "If this were you in your mother's place, would you want to be kept alive like this?" She said, "No, I would not." Then I asked, "What do you think your mother would want done if she could speak for herself?" "Oh, she would not want it," the daughter told me. A friend of mine who used to be a hospital chaplain at this point would tell people, "Sounds like your mother has already made up her mind. The question is whether you are going to honor it or not."

Another way we can honor those we love is by providing them with a comfortable and dignified death. When cure is no longer an option, a peaceful death can be a legitimate goal. What could it look like? Those dependent on us could be as pain-free as possible. They could be comforted by the presence of their family. If possible, they could be in familiar surroundings at home or in the nursing home. They could be touched and held and talked to and prayed for. They could have a chance to say good-bye to those they love and perhaps reconnect with those who have been estranged. They could be honored by allowing a natural death to occur. A natural death would not be distorted by aggressive medical procedures that offer no hope of recovery and only prolong the dying process.

> ✔ *I will honor the people I love by doing all within my power to keep them comfortable and by honoring their wishes regarding medical treatment decisions.*

Modern Medicine and "the Enemy"

> The last enemy to be destroyed is death. Death
> has been swallowed up in victory. Where, O death, is
> your victory? Where, O death, is your sting?
>
> *I Corinthians 15:26, 54-55*

Well, there you have it. The scripture says it. Death is the enemy. Perhaps we should make a better choice of enemies. Think about it. The death expectancy rate is one hundred percent. I fear that much of the practice of medicine also sees death as the only enemy, in spite of the fact that all of us die. Our medical schools, the physicians they produce, and the hospitals they practice in have set themselves up for failure if the only good outcome is anything but death. Death is *an* enemy but not the *only* enemy.

Is the practice of medicine wrong in fighting death? Of course not... most of the time. But we, as patients and our families, are not served by fighting death when we clearly know this battle will be lost. What medical science can do is enhance the quality of our lives in our last days. It can keep pain under control. Physicians, and other health professionals, can treat us with dignity, warmth, compassion, and caring. They cannot abandon us in the hour of our greatest need. They can know that they have not "failed" because I am dying. Just because I can't be cured does not mean modern medicine has nothing to offer.

I often ask people when they feel it would be appropriate to stop life-sustaining medical treatment. Most often they say something like, "When I don't have my right mind any more," or "When I can no longer recognize my family." Losing our mind to advanced dementia, or losing consciousness in the last stages of a terminal illness, seems to be a sign to most people of a "right time" to die. It is a time when death does not seem to cut off the possibility of further development.

Daniel Callahan writes,

> Death is acceptable, I contend, when it comes at the point in a life when (1) further efforts to defer dying are likely to deform the process of dying, or when (2) there is a good fit between the biological inevitability of death in general and the particular timing and circumstances of that death in the life of an individual. This dual standard does not imply that there is a perfect moment for death to occur; that may be an unnecessary fiction. It is necessary to think only in terms of death's falling within an acceptable range of possibilities.... A death is 'merciful' in its circumstances, or a 'blessing,' when in the life being lived the possibility of enjoying the goods of life has been forever lost.[20]

The hospice movement has shown us that death is not the only enemy, and death does not have to be horrible. When cure is no longer possible then we can expect our physicians and healthcare facilities to offer us the very best medicine. We can shift the focus from the disease to the patient. Shift from cure to comfort. More importantly, when our disease progresses to the point that physical healing is no longer possible, then we can focus on more important things. We can spend time with our family, do those things we want to get done, or attend to our spiritual life. By making death the only enemy and its defeat the only reasonable activity, we will miss fully living some of the most important days of our lives... our last ones.

✔ *When the time is right I will no longer fight death but battle to live each day as fully as possible.*

Willingness to Yield

Then I heard the voice of the Lord saying, "Whom shall I send, and who will go for us?" And I said, "Here am I; send me!"

Isaiah 6: 8

Then Jesus, crying with a loud voice, said, "Father, into your hands I commend my spirit." Having said this, he breathed his last.

Luke 23: 46

There is no greater task in the shadow of a life-threatening illness than finally letting go in grace and trust rather than holding on out of fear.

The couple had been married for more than sixty years. Now he lay still, brought low by a stroke. She was regularly at his side in the nursing home. For four years he made no movement, no eye contact, nothing to indicate he was aware of his surroundings. His life was sustained by food and water artificially being supplied through a feeding tube.

Two years into his nursing home stay, I gave her my newly published booklet *Hard Choices for Loving People*. She sought me out to talk about it. She was touched by the possibility of stopping the artificial feeding and allowing her husband to die a natural death. As we sat in the chapel, she said, "I have not been able to sleep since reading your book." We talked at length. I told her we could talk about it at any time, but I would not initiate this subject again. This decision had to be hers, because she would have to live peacefully with it.

For two more years neither she nor I brought up the subject again. But I felt compelled to break my promise and ask her to revisit the withdrawal of artificial measures. Her husband's condition had now declined to the point that his leg broke as he was routinely turned by his nurses. Also, she herself had been in and out of the hospital, and I feared that if anything happened to her, this man would be forever trapped without someone feeling empowered to release him.

We talked and we prayed. Once, as we walked to his room she said, "I know my husband would never want to be kept alive like this. I know it would be best if he just died. I know he is never going to get better. But I just can't let go."

In spite of her great struggle, she did move toward releasing him. She indicated she wanted to order the withdrawal of the artificial feeding. One of our nursing home administrators and I set up a meeting with her. We had prepared a document for her to sign authorizing the withdrawal of treatment.

When she arrived for the meeting she brought a professional person with her—not a lawyer, not a doctor. She had asked her minister to be with her at this meeting. The message to me was that she knew this was neither a medical nor a legal decision but a spiritual one.

The administrator and I briefly reviewed the case and assured the wife that her husband would be comfortable in his dying if she ordered the withdrawal of the artificial feedings. The pastor asked if we would give him a few minutes to speak to the woman alone. We left. In a few minutes he asked us to come back into the room. The wife said she had decided to stop the artificial feeding, and she signed the document. Her next words were, "I feel like a great burden has been lifted from my shoulders." She had let go.

✔ *The beginning point of this process of letting go is being willing to yield to forces beyond myself. May I begin to practice a willingness to yield today.*

Four

The Journey to Letting Be

Putting it together

> [A child] avoids [despair] by building defenses; and these defenses allow him to feel a basic sense of self-worth, of meaningfulness, of power. They allow him to feel that he controls his life and his death, that he really does live and act as a willful and free individual, that he has a unique and self-fashioned identity, that he is somebody.... We don't want to admit that we are fundamentally dishonest about reality, that we do not really control our own lives.[21]
>
> *Ernest Becker*

A couple of summers ago I was wandering through an arts festival in Crested Butte, Colorado, and I came across the works of an artist who made pencil drawings. I was fascinated by one of his sketches he had made of his two-year-old son depicting him as if the image were an unfinished jigsaw puzzle. The child is looking down at his hand emerging from the flat surface of the drawing with a piece of the puzzle in his grasp. He is searching for the place where that one piece of himself fits. The artist titled the picture "Putting it Together."[22] Surely the task of a two-year-old is to figure out who he or she is.

I saw that drawing and said to myself, "This is where our struggle with dying starts." We work so hard from day one creating an ego... a self... a personality... a person who has a healthy self-image and can function in the world. And yet we come to our last days and realize that we must let go of this life's work.

It is natural and necessary for children, adolescents, and even adults to build strong, healthy egos. This task of creating a healthy self-image is undertaken to gain control of ourselves and the world around us.

Ever since our ancestors first walked upright the human race has struggled to gain control. At first it was the basics like building a fire, finding shelter, and gathering food. Gaining control has led us today to having air conditioning and restaurants. (I don't want to go back to caves and eating grubs and roots.) I am glad our species has progressed in so many ways.

In a sense, every child makes his or her own progress and gains a feeling of control. This positive self-image that gives us a feeling of being in control, and therefore safe, allows us to grow and thrive. What is truly happening is that WE are creating this ego. We are making ourselves with the material that is handed to us genetically and emotionally. If we do the job adequately, we can live a life with emotional and spiritual health.

So why did the picture of the child make me think, "This is where our struggle with dying starts"? Sadly, in the last phase of life, all this meticulously constructed personality we created is revealed for what is it... a mask. As a matter of fact, the root meaning of the words person and personality is from the Latin *persona,* which was a mask worn by actors in a play.

When we gain a sense that our time on earth is short, either because of the diagnosis of a terminal illness or just from an internal awareness that our end is near, the mask of ego begins to peel away. We may appear the same and probably even express ourselves in ways we always have, but the importance we once put on our "self," our "person," is lessened. Confronting the false nature of our self is painful.

> In a sense, it s not so much just that the prognosis [of a terminal disease] is a tragedy, but that the integration of the news of prognosis reveals our tragic state. Stephen Levine speaks of the fear of death as "the imagined loss of imagined individuality."... One woman, dying of cancer, referred to her disease and the process of dying as an "ego-ectomy."[23]

You might think, "Why go to all this trouble and build a strong self? You are going to die anyway." Funny thing, the emotionally healthiest among us have the easiest time letting go of this carefully constructed person. Not that it is easy by any means. But it is only when we are strong that we can face the reality that this persona will fade away. Usually, realizing and accepting the false nature of the ego is accompanied with a sense of being part of a greater whole. This is true not only for those who believe in God but for anyone who is reconciled to the fact that death is inevitable.

> ✔ *While I am grateful for the person I have become and this self has brought me so far, I shall have the courage to recognize the fragile nature of my own creation.*

"It doesn't matter"

> The spiritual path, as Meister Eckhart observed, has more to do with subtraction than with addition. It is not so much a matter of adding all the active virtues to one's practice of living as of relinquishing everything that can possibly be abandoned.[24]
>
> *Belden Lane*
>
> The only way to live in any security is to live so close to the bottom that when you fall you do not have far to drop, you do not have much to lose.[25]
>
> *Dorothy Day*

My father spent the last four-and-a-half years of his life in a nursing home. And for years before the nursing home, his health made a slow decline as a result of Parkinson's disease and strokes. Dad had been a person with a quick mind. He authored eighteen books on various aspects of Florida history and traveled the state lecturing on the subject.

After his retirement from his day job at age seventy, Dad spent a few years presenting short "historical moments" on a local TV station once a week. He loved going on location where he would tell his viewers what had happened on the spot where he was standing. He got paid for his work but he told me once, "They don't know it, but I would do it for free it is so much fun."

A year or so after his nursing home admission, we picked him up so he could go for a ride with us. I was driving, Dad was in the passenger seat, and my mother and nephew were in the back. We stopped at a traffic light where, across the street, stood a fire tower that once was used to spot fires in the forest on land that now was covered with suburban sprawl. The tower was closed and fenced in with an historical marker telling its story.

From the back seat Mom said, "Your dad did a TV spot on that corner." Dad immediately corrected her, saying, "I did several!" With the light still red I asked a question to pass the time, "Dad when was that tower last used to spot forest fires?" He started thinking and searching his disease-damaged brain for the date that was locked in there somewhere. But he could not find it. Knowing dates and times and places were things that had been important to my father. He lived and breathed Florida history. Now the ravages of his own aging had robbed him of the ability to give me the date.

Dad had to make a choice of what to do with this moment. The light was still red and no date came to mind. Slowly he turned and with a big grin he said, "It doesn't matter!" He smiled, seemingly satisfied that losing the date was okay. At an earlier time it mattered greatly.

All his adult life dad had gathered old photographs, postcards, newspaper articles, and other historical documents about Florida. The collection was quite valuable to those researching related topics. There was so much "stuff" that my parents built an additional room on the house to store it. Years before he started declining he made a commitment that upon his death all this material would be given to the university. And when his hands could no longer hold a book or turn a page or type a sentence, he told Mom to call the university and have them start taking the documents away.

I asked him once, after he was in the nursing home, what it was like calling the university and having them take his life's work away. He burst into tears and said, "It was the hardest thing I ever did." Here was a man who had grown up during the Great Depression, lost his father at age ten, served in Europe during World War II, buried a seven-day-old child, and raised three teenagers through the '60s… and the hardest thing he ever did was let go of the materials he labored over for his entire working life.

Dad was right on schedule. If we have not started the process of relinquishing our attachment to things earlier in our life, then the task is forced upon us in the last phase of life. Of course my father's "things" had the additional emotional overlay of being the symbol of his labor of love over a lifetime. We hope the work of our life will benefit future generations, as did my father's. But as far as giving us personal value now, especially at the end of life, it doesn't matter.

This is the mirror image of the child putting the pieces of the puzzle of his life together. My father was learning what was on a list of items that don't really matter, in the grand scheme of things. They were once important bits of history that, when collected together, formed books or two minutes a week on TV. In a sense it is like putting the pieces of the puzzle back in the box.

I don't mean to imply that the things we once cherished have value no longer. We especially are aware of this when we usually consider what is most important—our family and the love we share. In the last phase of life, it becomes pretty clear that things material have less value than things spiritual. People are more important than possessions. Even worthwhile endeavors, like a profession or charity work, begin to fade in importance.

I once was visiting a woman in her early sixties who was in the last days of a life shortened by acute leukemia. She was a college professor and delighted in helping the students learn. As a matter of fact, when she was first diagnosed with a more chronic form of the disease, she continued teaching for a couple of years. She was now in a hospital bed near a window that looks out from her home onto a lake. I asked her if she had any regrets about her life.

She said, "I wish I had quit my job as soon as I was diagnosed. I am too sick now to do things with my grandchildren. I could have traveled with my husband. I felt it was so important to go on doing the work I loved. I missed an opportunity."

Others make the choice to continue work and seem satisfied with it. I knew another professor at the same college who felt it was so important to continue teaching, even though he was ravaged with cancer, that he fought through his weakness and taught up until the day before he died.

After we get to some level of acceptance with the grief of having to let go of so many things that in their time mattered greatly, this can be a very liberating time of life. We can truly focus on what is most important. We can accept ourselves for who we are rather than for what we do. As our list of what matters most gets shorter, our burdens get lighter.

✔ *When I begin to recognize that much of what I have held most dear really doesn't matter, may I also have a sense that I am part of something so much greater.*

Idol of Control

> Self-respect and integrity need not, and ideally ought not, to be grounded in a capacity to control our lives and mortality.... We do ourselves a great and double harm by focusing the meaning of self-determination, and the shaping of a self, on our capacity to make external choices, to act.[26]
>
> *Daniel Callahan*

On a Monday morning I received two voice mail messages, one from a social worker and one from a nurse on my hospice team. They both essentially said, "We have a new patient, living in her daughter's home, who is very close to dying (In fact, she was within five days of dying, but we did not know that at the time.). She is frail, totally dependent on others for care, and was just released from the hospital after they were able to wean her off a ventilator. The daughter says she wants everything done to keep her mother alive including resuscitation attempts and once again the use of machines to maintain her breathing. The patient does not have the capacity to make her own decisions. Can you help us?"

When I finally got to the home I met this incapacitated lady who was lying in a recliner chair in her daughter's family room. She could not speak or lift a hand but seemed to acknowledge my presence. With the daughter talking for her mother, I gathered the usual information a chaplain does in assessing the pastoral care needs of the patient and her family. After a prayer I asked the daughter if she could follow me to the car because I wanted to give her a copy of my book on end-of-life decisions.

Standing outside we talked briefly about what I understood to be her wishes that everything be done to keep her mother from dying. She said she had indicated that. She added that she really did not want all those heroic measures, but she just did not want to make these decisions ahead of time and therefore lose control of the situation. Then, with tears in her eyes, she said, "All I want is for my mother to die peacefully here at home."

I told her we at hospice could help her with that but it wouldn't involve calling the rescue squad, CPR, or a machine to breathe for her mom. I advised her that dying peacefully at home takes a lot of planning and preparation. Ending up in the ICU hooked up to machines, for most people, is the accident we never intended for our last hours. This daughter, who had said she did not want to lose control, was able to shift her thinking. On Saturday, her mother died peacefully with her family gathered around.

Control appears to be the number one task for us in the world. We all like to be in control. Advertisers often tell us that their product or service "puts you in control." They know how important this is to us so they entice us with the notion that if we buy their brand we have more command of our lives. There is good reason this desire to be in charge is so important.

When we feel in control, life works better for us. An organized house and workplace allows us to function more efficiently. Traffic lights and road signs keep the vehicles moving in a safe and orderly manner. Most people feel they need to keep their weight within reasonable limits, which in turn makes us healthier. Many illnesses and medical conditions can be cured or in some way controlled, thus extending our lives and often raising our quality of life. Pain management has advanced, and there is less physical suffering. Who could fault the human race for these improvements when there are wonderful benefits derived from our desire to manage the world around us.

The ability to sometimes have power over a disease is one of the reasons why illness in general and a life-threatening illness in particular are so hard for us. To be unable to "defeat" the disease causes us to we feel like we are losing control. In addition to the physical discomfort of the sickness is the emotional struggle brought on by the apparent loss of control.

The losses associated with advanced illness are reminders of the loss of control. The loss of the ability to walk, the loss of the freedom to drive a car, and the loss of control of our bodily functions are just a few examples of slowly losing our grasp on a very normal desire to manage our lives.

As he faced his own imminent death with cancer, Charles Schulz, the creator of the cartoon "Peanuts," said to his friend and fellow cartoonist Lynn Johnston, "Isn't it amazing how you have no control over your real life? You control all these characters and the lives they live. You decide when they get up in the morning, when they're going to fight with their friends, when you're going to lose the game."[27]

But of our own real life, he says, we have no control.

As a pastoral care giver to those in the midst of such struggles, I have often found myself at a loss for words that can offer comfort. Sometimes I borrow words from the play "W;t" spoken by a nurse to a terminally ill patient and all I can say is, "It's like it's out of control, isn't it?"[28] Somehow, one can feel solace just knowing a fellow human being at least recognizes the utter frustration of the experience. It doesn't necessarily take away the pain, but at least someone knows what we are going through.

Sr. Elaine M. Prevallet, S.L., helped me put a label on the downside of the effort to always be in charge. She writes,

> The idol of control holds out to us the hope that suffering and death can be eliminated. If we just get smart enough, we will gain control of pain and even of death. That false hope, in turn,

has the effect of setting suffering up as an enemy to be avoided at all costs. We can choose never to suffer!... Power, particularly perceived as domination or control, is, I believe, our cultural idol.... The idol requires that we devote our time and energy, our hearts and souls, to keeping this illusion alive. And we do.[29]

Let me first say that I do not believe that anyone in physical pain should not hope for and receive relief through medications or other treatments. I have been told by experts in the field that with advanced illness, pain can be controlled. Nor do I feel attempts to completely cure a disease in its early and middle stages are in any way misguided. But these are efforts to have power over physical pain and of the illness itself.

The emotional and spiritual suffering that follows the feeling of the loss of control is more profound. In our culture, we have made a sort of idol of being in control. When our loss of function and our impending death force us to face the fact that there are some things beyond our control, we despair. This quality of influencing and even manipulating the events of our lives that has served us so well up to the point of a life-threatening illness has now let us down.

We usually think of an idol as something we worship. In monotheistic religions (e.g., Islam, Judaism, or Christianity) an idol is any object of worship other than the one God. Although there are times when seeking to have command of a situation is appropriate, it can become idolatry. We must judge whether we have made the shift from a normal and healthy desire to direct events to making control an idol.

Simply put, any attempt to have mastery over something that is beyond control can be considered idolatrous. The daughter in the story I related said she wanted her mother hooked up to machines and wanted to be in charge of all decisions. Like the ancients who worshipped a block of wood to perform a miracle, sometimes modern medicine is used in situations for which it was never intended and we find ourselves in the stance of worshipping it. Is our attempt to gain control an attempt to place an action above God (if one believes in God)? If it is, then for us that act of control becomes an idol. Turns out this daughter didn't really want to stop something beyond her ability to influence—the fact that her mother was going to die sooner rather than later—and she made a choice to control what she could, a peaceful passing.

If we find ourselves worshipping the idol of control, what do we do? We have to come to terms with our own limitations. We have to accept those things that we can't control. We don't have to accept them as "good" necessarily, but we must acknowledge that they are real and we can't change them. We can still control the controllable things even while we "accept with serenity the things that cannot be changed."

> ✔ At those times when I try to dominate things beyond my control, I shall confess my own worshipping at the idol of control and once again seek the serenity to accept things I cannot change.

Letting Be Is the Next Step

> To let go is to lose your foothold temporarily. Not to let go is to lose your foothold forever.[30]
>
> *Søren Kierkegaard*

While I was working on the 4th Edition of *Hard Choices for Loving People* I sought advice on the manuscript from a number of people. I get to a final version of my books by writing a draft and then sending it around to experts, fellow workers, and friends to give me feedback. Joanne Lynn, MD, has always offered wonderful suggestions for improving whatever I have written. Next to my poem "Giving Up and Letting Go" she wrote, "I have started using the term 'letting be' and dropping 'letting go.'"

Well! How dare she mess with my very popular poem. Furthermore, I was about to go to press and I didn't want to start fiddling with what took me a long time to refine. So there! I'm not changing it.

As time has passed I have ruminated over her words. My own personal spiritual and philosophical outlook on life has also moved toward letting be. Letting be acknowledges that what is, is. It is a stance of acceptance. As gentle as I feel "letting go" is, for some people, it still implies losing something. Many people hear the words "letting go" and they immediately recoil thinking it means loss or dying. I know when I was originally writing *Light in the Shadows* I had considered a title that featured the words "letting go." But I rejected the idea since the seriously ill people I was trying to reach might never pick up the book because of the negative baggage some attach to letting go.

So here it is. It's not perfect, but it does reflect where my head is on the subject right now.

Giving Up and Letting Go and Letting Be

Giving up implies a struggle —
Letting go implies a partnership —
Letting be implies, in reality, there is nothing that separates

Giving up says there is something to lose —
Letting go says there is something to gain —
Letting be says it doesn't matter

Giving up dreads the future —
Letting go looks forward to the future —
Letting be accepts the present as the only moment I ever have

Giving up lives out of fear —
Letting go lives out of grace and trust —
Letting be just lives

Giving up is defeat —
Letting go is victory —
Letting be knows suffering is often in my own mind in the first place

Giving up is unwillingly yielding control to forces beyond myself —
Letting go is choosing to yield to forces beyond myself —
Letting be acknowledges that control and choices can be illusions

Giving up believes that God is to be feared —
Letting go trusts in God to care for me —
Letting be never asks the question

Of course I am not the first one to talk this way. Here are a few of my guides:

> The expressions *letting go* and *releasing* suggest a specific act with a specific object. On the other hand, the words *yielding* and *allowing* seem to name an inner posture, an undergirding orientation. But yielding has not always gotten good press. "Yielding to a sin," as an old revival hymn puts it. The words refer to yielding to temptation, of course, but somehow they do reflect our cultural bias: to be in control is to be strong; to yield is to be weak.... Yielding seems to involve first a fundamental attitude of receptivity, a willingness to enter life as it presents itself to us, to embrace what *is*.[31]

> Surrender is a stance of the whole being in which resistance, at any level, ceases as one willingly becomes active in *what is*.

Surrender is not so much *agreeing to,* but *agreeing with.* With surrender, we cease being a victim of life.[32]

After acceptance, surrender. It is the surrender of the self into the present. One nurse, Janet Quinn, who has worked extensively with AIDS patients, had this to say: "Surrendering is incredibly empowering because it is an action and giving up is the refusal to take action. Giving up is saying there's nothing else to do.... To surrender is absolutely active and requires doing over and over again. Surrender is not something that's done once and for all.... It's required minute by minute. Being surrendered is becoming extraordinarily active in one's process.... Surrender increases the quality of life... and the quality of one's dying. There is peacefulness that comes with that... versus the despair that comes with giving up."[33]

✔ *I shall begin to practice letting be by accepting what is.*

May My Suffering Relieve Someone Else's

> Suffering ceases to be suffering at the moment it finds a meaning, such as the meaning of a sacrifice.[34]
>
> *Viktor Frankl*

Ruth was an emaciated shadow of an eighty-year-old. Her frail frame with flesh stretched over her thin bones couldn't have weighed ninety pounds. She had been reduced to a bed-to-chair existence as a result of respiratory failure. Constantly on oxygen, it took her a half hour to recover from the move to the bed from the chair not two feet away. In spite of all this I can never remember her without a smile and something witty to say.

I asked her once, "How do you keep so happy with all the physical problems you have?" Without missing a beat she responded, "Oh. There are so many people so much worse off than I am." She smiled.

I am guessing she lived her whole life with this attitude. You don't get to the last phase of life, confined to a second-floor room, barely able to breathe, and all of a sudden develop a generous spirit toward the plight of someone else. But you can begin to practice keeping others in mind as you contemplate your own situation. Here are two suggestions for taking your own life situation and using it on behalf of others. These are suggestions for giving and receiving.

First let us consider a time when we are painfully aware of our own suffering… when our ability to function declines… or the pain increases… or when we are almost overwhelmed with the thought that life as we know it will soon end. In that moment of despair, bring to mind someone you love who also suffers either from a medical condition or an emotional pain like grieving, or struggling with a divorce, or someone experiencing financial setbacks. In the moment of your own hurt you might think, or even whisper softly, "May my suffering help identify more with the suffering of this person I love."

Does this "work" in reducing the other's suffering? I don't know. But it certainly can transform the meaning of our own pain.

> Viktor Frankl wrote we "are not destroyed by suffering. We are destroyed by suffering without meaning." He is also fond of quoting Nietzsche, "He who has a *why* to live can bear with almost any *how*."[35]

I can't tell you the number of times frail and failing patients have told me that they know they are still on earth for a purpose. We humans have a drive from deep within our souls to find meaning. We also have the unique ability to transform a moment of suffering into a moment lived on behalf of others.

Which brings me to a second way of transforming a moment in time. We all have occasions, I hope, when life is good. Not that we have no problems but, for a while, we recognize a space of joy in the midst of our suffering. Perhaps a friend tells us a joke… or today's pain is less than yesterday's… or we see the flowers for the first time in the spring… any one of life's little pleasures. In that instant bring to mind again another who suffers and think or quietly whisper, "May my joy go out to the person I love and give them a better day."

Again, Viktor Frankl reflecting on his experience in the Nazi concentration camps:

> I spoke of our sacrifice, which had meaning in every case. It was in the nature of this sacrifice that it should appear to be pointless in the normal world, the world of material success. But in reality our sacrifice did have a meaning. Those of us who had any religious faith, I said frankly, could understand without difficulty. I told them of a comrade who on his arrival in camp had tried to make a pact with Heaven that his suffering and death should save the human being he loved from a painful end. For this man,

suffering and death were meaningful; his was a sacrifice of the deepest significance. He did not want to die for nothing. None of us wanted that.[36]

> ✔ *May any joy I am privileged to experience go out to bring joy to others and may any suffering that is mine serve to bring me closer to the agony in one I love.*

True Solace Is Finding None

> What the desert teaches is a radical letting-go
> of the thinking-experiencing-managing self, so as to
> be content with God alone, a God without adjectives,
> without comforting signs of presence, so that at last
> one learns truly to delight in nothing.[37]
>
> *Belden C. Lane*
>
> Enlightenment for a wave is the moment the
> wave realizes that it is water. At that moment, all fear
> of death disappears.[38]
>
> *Thich Nhat Hanh*

Sometimes nothing seems to help. Nothing takes away the emotional pain of this moment. The grief of a lost love or the reality of my own death loom so large, the ache is so great, all answers fail. People can feel abandoned, alone, like no one in the universe is watching out for their best interest.

The religions of the world often like to offer solutions to this emotional and spiritual pain. Whether one of the "great religions" or the latest self-help book, the formula goes something like "do this and all will be better." It is not unusual that at the bedside of a terminally ill person I have heard, "I don't know how people get through this without a faith in God." They are truly comforted. Their faith has been a great source of strength.

Yet there are times, even for the most faithful, when God doesn't seem to be keeping up God's end of the bargain. The formula seems to fail. You read, "If in my name you ask me for anything, I will do it."[39] But after praying earnestly for healing, the disease continues to move forward.

I have been so greatly helped by Kathleen Dowling Singh, a hospice social worker, who has put words on what is so beyond words. In *The Grace in Dying: how we are transformed spiritually as we die,* she has shed light on this movement out of the despair of nothing helping toward love and grace at the end of life.

> The tragedy of the loss of me,… is transformed into grace. Tragedy holds the seeds of grace.… Grace is the experience of the finally, gratefully, relaxing of the contraction of fearful separation and opening to Spirit as our own radiant splendor: knowing it, feeling it, entering it, as it enters us.[40]

> It is a movement from personality to soul to Spirit. We remember who we are, paradoxically, by forgetting, by retracing the steps that led to the creation of the mental ego. The fourteenth-century contemplative Christian document The *Cloud of the Unknowing* reminds us that the only way back to union with God is "forgetting, forgetting, forgetting." This is the emptying of self.[41]

Nothing. Can there be comfort in nothing? When divine help seems so far away, how does one get through? Ironically, these same great religions that promise comfort to the believer, also have a side that says sometimes nothing is all you need. Often this thinking has come from the fringe of the religion. Either the desert monastics or the martyrs gain great support from no apparent support. But it is not just the religious types who have made this discovery of comfort in nothingness.

Gretel Ehrlich, a former TV producer from New York, chronicles her life in the harsh ranching lifestyle of her adopted Wyoming. She tells a great story about being most comforted at a point when nothing seemed to help. Her fiancé had just died and she was going through the ups and downs of grief. Nothing seemed to help alleviate the sadness.

> One morning a couple in a car from New York drove by. "Ah…" they must have thought, "a real cowgirl." As the car slowed to go through town I found myself trotting behind it. I wanted to pound on the windows and explain that I knew every subway

stop on the Seventh Avenue IRT. They speeded up and drove on. I laughed at myself, then went inside and wrote to a friend: "True solace is finding none, which is to say, it is everywhere."[42]

This is so hard to explain. The idea that when all support, comfort, and solace is gone then we are most consoled, is beyond words. Words actually get in the way. Those who have come to believe that in nothing we have everything often come to that conclusion out of the silence. Somehow, when stripped of outward signs of comfort, they find the ultimate serenity. No one tells them how. They do not read it in a book. They just become convinced from deep within that they are part of something so much greater than themselves.

Irony of ironies, when there is no apparent support, we can be overwhelmed with grace and love. At a time when all seems lost we are left with pure love. We have come full circle from the child putting the puzzle together when trying to figure out who he is. In the end, we put the pieces of the self we created back in the box. There is no self, no personality, no ego. We are free.

✔ *May my last phase of life complete the process of letting go of my own created ego in favor of seeing myself as a part of something so much greater.*

Conclusion

Light Amidst the Shadows

As Buddha said: "What you are is what you have been, what you will be is what you do now." Another teacher went further: "If you want to know your past life, look into your present condition; if you want to know your future life, look at your present actions."[43]

Sogyal Rinpoche

On my first and last visit into Jane's home, I was greeted in the living room by her husband and a woman who was a close family friend. Jane was within days of dying and was in the bedroom. The husband and friend filled me in on the situation before we moved to the bedside. I stood on one side of the bed and Jane's husband knelt at the other side, taking her hand. The friend stood behind him. Jane was so weak I could hardly hear her voice. At one point she looked to her husband and said, "I love you." I asked if they would like to have a prayer, and we held hands making a circle including this dying woman. After I ended my prayer the husband asked if we could say the "Lord's Prayer" and I said yes. We concluded the prayer and I left the room.

I was hardly at the bedside five minutes, ten at the most. I could offer only the bare minimum to this failing patient and her loving family. I walked into the living room to wait and have a few last words with the family when this friend emerged from the bedroom. She came up to me, threw her arms around me and said, "You are so wonderful. That was just what we needed. You have helped so much." My first thought was, "Boy, is this job easy." And my very next thought was, "What a privilege to be here at such an important moment in the life of this family. I am so fortunate to be able to learn so many of life's lessons by walking with others through these difficult times."

People say to me, "Oh. You work for hospice. That must be depressing.... Hospice workers are so special." Whether it's at a party, or in the grocery checkout line, or with a family member at the bedside, this is often the comment I get when someone discovers I am a hospice chaplain.

I've got some news for all who believe this myth. First, we are not so special. I feel I am not different from any other human being. Perhaps it is this realization that I am not different, and that one day I will be in that bed looking up at another hospice chaplain, that has helped me do this work.

The other piece of news is that this work is only sometimes depressing. My life is so much richer because of time spent with those who have a life-threatening illness and their families. Out of the shadows of the individual tragedies I witness comes a great light. Sickness and death are always sad. And surely these patients and families would have wished things to be different. But it is out of sufferings that we can learn much about living.

What have I learned and what can I share with others?

I have learned to live my life with so much more gratitude, like Mary, who said being blind was wonderful.

I have learned from the man who felt guilty when his son died because he had so much more to tell him. What I learned is not to let a day go by when I haven't said all I want to say to my family and friends.

I have learned that even in the darkest hour a sense of humor can bring light, like the man who had such an unusual illness that there were only eight known cases like his. When I asked him how he felt to have such a rare disease, through a big grin he said, "Special!" He died on Christmas Day.

I have learned that you can let go of someone you love dearly, like the fifteen-year-old girl whose mother was dying of cancer. She had already been abandoned by her father but was able to tell her mother, "I am going to be okay. I am going to have a good life. You can go now." The mother who had fought for months to hold on for her children died a few hours later.

I have learned I have a choice in how I respond to any set of circumstances like the forty-two-year-old MS patient who had no sense of bitterness over the unfairness of being cut down before his time.

I have learned that I must practice "letting go" and living peacefully my whole life if I hope to come to the end of my days like my Aunt Nell, who died gently because she lived gently.

I have learned to sense the presence of God in the most difficult circumstances, like the woman dying in the concentration camp hearing the words, "I am here. I am life—eternal life."

I have learned that one day everything will be taken away from me—my health, my home, my family, my career, my possessions—so today I must nurture the things that will last. I want to give attention daily to my inward spiritual life and to the love I share with others. Not wanting to be caught off-guard, I often ask myself, "Is today the day?"

I have learned that although I know it will be a sad day, I can accept my own death as being right, like my aunt, who said, "It's my time."

End Notes

1. Hank Dunn, Hard Choices for Loving People: CPR, Artificial Feeding, Comfort Care and the Patient with a Life-Threatening Illness, Fourth Ed. Herndon, VA: A & A Publishers, 2001.

2. Melody Beattie, The Language of Letting Go: Daily Meditations for Codependents, New York: HarperCollins, 1990, p. 46.

3. Reynolds Price, A Whole New Life: An Illness and a Healing, New York: Atheneum, 1994, pp. 53, 184-185.

4. Harold S. Kushner, When Bad Things Happen to Good People, New York: Avon Books, 1981, pp. 51-53.

5. Ibid., Beattie, p. 320.

6. Lewis B. Smedes, The Art of Forgiving: When You Need to Forgive and Don't Know How, Nashville: Moorings/ Random House, 1996, pp. 177-178.

7. Morrie Schwartz, Letting Go: Morrie's Reflections on Living While Dying, Walker and Co., 1996, pp. 51-52.

8. Viktor E. Frankl, Man's Search for Meaning, New York: Washington Square Press, 1984, pp. 86-87.

9. Sogyal Rinpoche, The Tibetan Book of Living and Dying, New York: Harper San Francisco, 1992, p. 33.

10. C.S. Lewis, A Grief Observed, New York: Seabury Press, Inc., 1961, p. 1.

11. Ibid., Schwartz, p. 13.

12. Ibid., Frankl, p. 90.

13. Ibid., Beattie, pp. 56-57.

14. Michel de Montaigne, The Essays: A Selection, New York: Penguin Books USA, 1987, p. 24.

15. Etty Hillesum, An Interrupted Life: The Diaries, 1941-1943 and Letters from Westerbork, New York: Henry Holt and Co., 1996, pp.153, 155.

16. Rainer Maria Rilke, Rilke's Book of Hours: Love Poems to God, trans: Anita Barrows and Joanna Macy, New York: Riverhead Books, 1996, p. 131.

17. Daniel Callahan, The Troubled Dream of Life: Living with Mortality, New York: Simon & Schuster, 1993, pp. 149, 151, 221.

18. Reinhold Niebuhr, "The Serenity Prayer," (1934), quoted in Familiar Quotations, 16th Edition, John Bartlett, Justin Kaplan, ed., Boston: Little, Brown and Company, 1992, p. 684.

19. Ibid., Schwartz, p. 30.

20. Ibid., Callahan, p. 149.

21. Ernest Becker, The Denial of Death. New York:The Free Press, 1973, p.55.

22. "Putting it Together" by J.D. Hillberry, JDH Art, 303-469-0059, www.JDHArt.com.

23. Kathleen Dowling Singh, The Grace in Dying: how we are transformed spiritually as we die, New York: HarperCollins, 1998, pp. 90, 161.

24. Belden C. Lane, The Solace of Fierce Landscapes: Exploring Desert and Mountain Spirituality. New York: Oxford University Press, 1999, p. 166.

25. Dorothy Day, "Poverty Is To Care and Not To Care," The Catholic Worker, April 1953, vol. 1, issue 5.

26. Ibid., Callahan, pp. 127-129.

27. "Cartoonists Mourn Charles Schulz," Associated Press, Feb. 13, 2000.

28. Margaret Edson, W;t, New York: Faber and Faber, Inc., 1999, p. 65.

29. Elaine M. Prevallet, S.L., "Borne in Courage and Love: Reflections on Letting Go" Weavings, March/April, 1997. pp. 11, 14.

30. Søren Kierkegaard, quoted in Singh, p. 155.

31. Ibid. Prevallet, p. 8.

32. Ibid, Singh, p. 158.

33. Dennis Gersten, "Interview with Janet Quinn: AIDS, Hopes, Healing, Part II," Atlantis (February 1992):3, quoted in Singh, p. 159.

34. Ibid., Frankl, p. 135.

35. Gordon W. Allport in the Introduction to Man's Search for Meaning, by Frankl, p 12.

36. Ibid., Frankl, p 104-105.

37. Ibid., Lane, p. 225.

38. Thich Nhat Hanh, quoted in Singh, p. 281.

39. John 14:14, New Revised Standard Version Bible, National Council of Churches of Christ, 1989.

40. Ibid., Singh, pp. 110-111.

41. Ibid., Singh, p. 274.

42. Gretel Ehrlich, The Solace of Open Spaces. New York: Penguin, 1985, p. 41.

43. Sogyal Rinpoche, Glimpse after Glimpse: Daily Reflections on Living and Dying, New York: HarperCollins, 1995, the reading for October 12.